All Around the Neighborhood

Piece O' Cake Designs, Inc.

Linda Jenkins and Becky Goldsmith
301 Handicap Avenue
Pagosa Springs, CO 81147

Acknowledgments

Every day we are thankful to all of those who have helped us make Piece O' Cake Designs a success. Our husbands, Steve Goldsmith and Paul Jenkins, willingly do anything that is asked of them. And, bless their hearts, they have become good at anticipating what we need before we need it.

Some of you have had the pleasure of visiting with our office staff. We could not do our job without them. Billi, our office manager, keeps everything running smoothly and efficiently. Kathleen handles the day in and day out details that help us to get our books and patterns to you — and they keep a smile on their faces every day. What a team!

Finally, we must acknowledge you, who buy and use our designs. Thank you so much for choosing to use our designs to make your own heirlooms.

Credits

Editor .... Steven Goldsmith
Photographer ....Chris Marona
Illustrations .... Becky Goldsmith
Quilts .... Linda Jenkins and Becky Goldsmith

All Around the Neighborhood
ISBN 0-9674393-1-0
© 1999 by Becky Goldsmith and Linda Jenkins
Piece O' Cake Designs, Inc.
301 Handicap Avenue
Pagosa Springs, CO 81147
Send a legal-size SASE for a complete Piece O' Cake catalog.

Table of Contents

Introduction

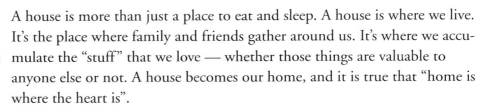

A house is more than just a place to eat and sleep. A house is where we live. It's the place where family and friends gather around us. It's where we accumulate the "stuff" that we love — whether those things are valuable to anyone else or not. A house becomes our home, and it is true that "home is where the heart is".

This book, <u>All Around the Neighborhood</u> is full of fun projects with a "house" theme. Linda's quilt, <u>All Around the Neighborhood</u>, is a bold bundle of houses surrounded by happy children. You can paint the houses in your quilted neighborhood to suit yourself (and don't we all wish our neighbors would consult us before they paint their houses?!)

<u>The Blessing Sampler</u> features Becky's favorite blessing. This charming wallhanging recalls the embroidered samplers of old while updating it for today's quilter.

The funky houses in <u>There Goes the Neighborhood</u> are pieced on the sewing machine and then appliqued in place. These blocks are embellished with a variety of beads and buttons.

Learn two different ways to piece a log cabin block. Linda's <u>Little Log Bungalows</u> are built with traditional piecing around a rectangular center. In <u>Windows Through the Cabin</u>, Becky chose an unconventional building technique that is easy and forgiving.

Be creative! Use these designs in other settings. You can do it! We have included line drawings of a few extra projects to get you started. Play with your colored pencils on these drawings to come up with new colorways that work in your own house. Small projects like pillows, placemats, and table runners are quick to make and fun to use. Leave a block unquilted and frame it for your wall. Make several houses and combine them with pieced blocks to make a bed quilt. The possibilities are endless.

With each new book we come up with more information for you! The instructions inside **All Around the Neighborhood** are for needleturn applique. Our book, **The Applique Handbook**, provides you with even more information on this method of hand applique. In it we have included instructions and many illustrations for techniques that you may not have tried before. However, please feel free to use your favorite applique technique to make your quilts. All of the projects in this book can be made using hand applique, machine applique, or fusible web with a stitched edge.

Supplies for Applique

It is important to have the right tools for the job at hand. This is as true in hand applique as it is in woodworking! Always use the best quality fabric, thread, and tools that you can afford. All fabrics and thread used in the quilts in this book are 100% cotton unless otherwise stated. We pre-wash our fabric. Following are important supplies that will make your stitching easier.

- Embroidery scissors
- Needles, straws or sharps
- 100% cotton thread to match your applique (DMC Broder Machine is our favorite thread for applique. If your local quilt shop doesn't carry this thread, contact us and we can help you find it.)
- White chalk pencil and mechanical pencil with 0.5 lead
- 1/2" sequin pins
- Permanent fine point marker to mark your overlays
- Clear upholstery vinyl for your overlays
- Clear self-laminating sheets (or clear, sticky shelf paper)
- Sandpaper board
- Bias bars for making the vine

General Applique Instructions

Prepare your backgrounds

Always cut your background fabric larger than the size it will be when it is pieced into the quilt. As you handle the block the outer edge can stretch and fray. Your applique can shift during stitching and can cause your block to shrink slightly. For these reasons it is best to add 1" to all sides of your backgrounds when you cut them out.

Press each background block in half vertically and horizontally. This establishes a center grid in your background that will line up with the center grid on your positioning overlay. Once your applique is complete, press each block and carefully trim it to size. Always make sure that your design is properly aligned with your ruler before you cut off the excess fabric.

Make your positioning overlays

The overlay is used to place each applique piece accurately into position. It is easy to make and use, and it makes your projects very portable. Cut a piece of clear upholstery vinyl, with its tissue paper lining, the finished size of each block. Using a ruler and a permanent fine point marker, draw a line down the horizontal and vertical center of the clear upholstery vinyl.

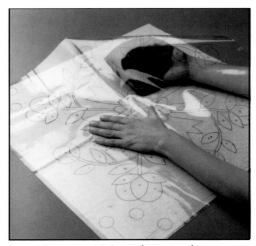

B/W Plate 1: Tracing the overlay   B/W Plate 2: Using the overlay

Lay this vinyl over the pattern, lining up the center grid on the vinyl with the one on the pattern. Trace the pattern accurately. The numbers on the pattern indicate stitching sequence. Include these numbers on your overlay (see above).

To use the overlay, lay your background right side up on your work surface. Place the overlay over it, also right side up. Line up the center grids. You will slide each applique piece, right side up, under the overlay but on top of the background one at a time. It is easy to see when the lines on your applique piece are in proper position under the overlay. We generally position and stitch one piece at a time. Remove the vinyl before stitching.

Making Templates

Each applique shape requires a template. We have a different way to make templates that we would like you to try. Make 2-5 copies of each block. From these copies cut out each shape that you need a template for. You do not need to cut them out neatly here. Leave some excess paper around them. Where one shape lays over another cut the top shape from one sheet and the bottom from another sheet. Some patterns have multiple pieces that lay over each other — this is what determines how many copies you will need.

Take one clear self-laminating sheet. Lay it shiny side down on the table in front of you. Peel the paper backing off which leaves the sticky side up. Carefully stick each template to the laminate, drawn side down (see illustration on page 9). Use more laminating sheets as necessary. Cut out each template.

You'll notice how easy these templates are to cut out. That is just one reason we like this method. Copies are usually more accuate than hand traced templates are. These templates are numbered on the copies. And, these templates are sturdy and hold up to multiple uses. What more could a quilter want!

There Goes the Neighborhood spices up any wall!
See instructions beginning on page 54.

All Around the Neighborhood is the focal point in this room.
Fabric and sewing tools let you know a quilter lives in this house!
See instructions beginning on page 10.

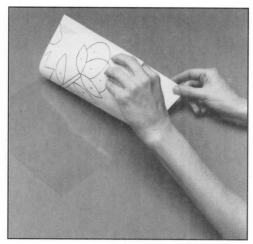

B/W Plate 3: Making templates

Using Templates

Lay your applique fabric right side up on a sandpaper board. The sandpaper keeps your fabric from shifting as you trace on it. Lay your template on the fabric, also right side up. Lay the template so that as many edges as possible are on the diagonal grain of the fabric. (A bias edge is easier to turn under than one that is on the straight of grain!) Trace around the template. Cut each piece out, adding a 3/16" seam allowance.

Finger press the edges of the applique pieces under before positioning them on your background to stitch. As you finger press, make sure that the drawn line is folded to the back. Cotton fabric has a magnificent memory! As you needleturn the seam allowances they will turn nicely along the finger pressed line.

Finish your quilt

After your applique is complete, press your blocks. Always iron your blocks on the reverse side. If your ironing surface is hard, lay your blocks on a towel and your applique will not get flattened. Trim your blocks to size. Assemble your quilt top.

We often put a corded edge on our quilts. The cording makes a nice, tailored edge. Additionally, the cording has a body that seems to help your quilts hang better. Make your cording and sew it to the quilt top before layering and basting. If you prefer a traditional bound edge, make it and add it after quilting is complete.

Layer and baste your quilt. Choose a batting that is suited to the finished product. Quilt your quilt. Finish the outer edge. Add hard embellishments once your quilting is complete.

Refer to our book, **The Applique Handbook**, if you would like even more information on needleturn applique.

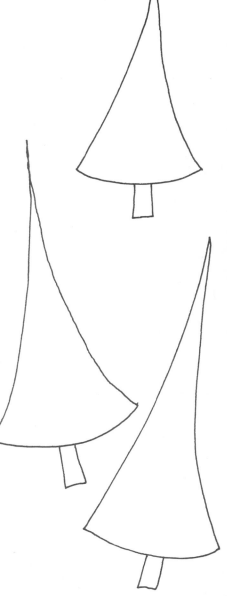

All Around the Neighborhood

Yardage for the 51" square wallhanging

See color photo on page 8.
Red Background: 1 1/2 yards
Black & White Checked Inner Border: 1/8 yard
Black Outer Border: 1 1/2 yards
Binding: one 25" square to make a continuous bias strip 2 1/2" wide -OR-
Cording: one 20" square to make a continuous bias strip 1 1/2" wide
Piping Cord: 5 3/4 yards
Backing and Sleeve: 3 1/3 yards
You will need a variety of small pieces of fabric for your applique.

Yardage for an 80" bed quilt

The drawing below shows one way to make more blocks into a bed quilt.
Background: 9 yards
5" Finished Outer Border: 1 1/4 yards (Cut eight 5 1/2" x 40 1/2" strips)
Binding: one 29" square to make a continuous bias strip 2 1/2" wide
Cording: one 24" square to make a continuous bias strip 1 1/2" wide
Piping Cord: 9 yards
Backing and Sleeve: 5 - 7 1/2 yards, depending on the width of your fabric
    after washing
You will need a variety of small pieces of fabric for your applique.

Let's sew up a neighborhood wallhanging!

Cut your background fabric as follows. The second measurement is the size to trim each block once your applique is complete.

Block #1 .... 17" x 13" — 15 1/2" x 11 1/2"
Block #2 .... 12" x 14" — 10 1/2" x 12 1/2"
Block #3 .... 12" square — 10 1/2" square
Block #4 .... 17" x 11" — 15 1/2" x 9 1/2"
Block #5 .... 12" square — 10 1/2" square
Block #6 .... 12" x 13" — 10 1/2" x 11 1/2"
Block #7 .... 17" x 14 1/2" — 15 1/2" x 13"
Block #8 .... 17" x 4 1/2" — 15 1/2" x 3"
Block #9 .... 12" x 14" — 10 1/2" x 12 1/2"
Block #10, the fence .... 12" x 15" — 10 1/2" x 13 1/2"
Block #11, the grass below Blocks 9 and 10 .... 20 1/2" x 1 1/2"
Inner Border .... Cut two 1" x 35 1/2" strips and two 1" x 36 1/2" strips
Borders .... Cut four 9 1/2" x 38" strips
Border Corners .... Cut four 9 1/2" squares

Use the applique directions on the preceding pages to make your quilt, or use your favorite applique method. Following are tips on cutaway applique, reverse applique, and circles that we hope you enjoy.

Cutaway applique on the roof edges

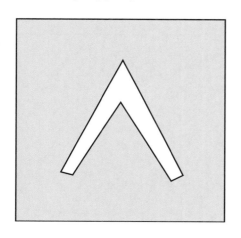

1. Place the roof-end (eave) template on top of the eave fabric, both right sides up. Be sure to lay the template on the fabric so that most of the edges will be on the diagonal grain of the fabric. Trace the eave.

2. Cut the eave out of the piece of eave fabric. Leave 1" or more of excess fabric around the traced stem. Be sure to leave the fabric intact between the two sides of the eave. Finger press the drawn line under.

3. Use your overlay to position the eave onto your block. Pin it in place. Position the pins on the outside edge of the eave.

5. The eave is being stitched. More fabric is trimmed away as you go. Clip the inner point when you can no longer turn the seam allowance under nicely.

4. Begin cutting away the excess fabric, leaving a 3/16" or smaller seam allowance. Stitch the inside edge of the eave first.

6. Remove the pins and stitch the second side of the eave. Clip away excess fabric as necessary.

Reverse Applique the Windows

1. Most of the windows on the houses are reverse appliqued. Begin with a piece of fabric for the wall (template #3) around the windows. Cut the windows out, leaving a rectangular hole for each. This piece of fabric needs to be 1" or so larger than the finished size of the wall.

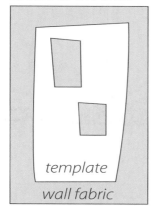

2. Use your overlay to position wall template #3. Trace around it. Also trace the window openings. Finger press the window edges.

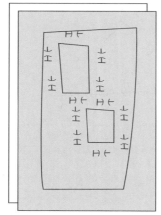

3. Lay the wall fabric over a piece of the window fabric. Pin the two fabrics together. Place your pins 1/4" away from the windows' edge.

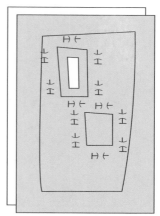

4. Cut out the excess fabric from inside one window. Leave a 3/16" seam allowance.

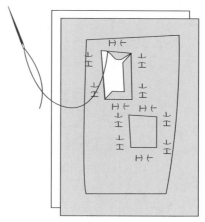

5. Needleturn the seam allowance under and stitch, clipping the corners as necessary.

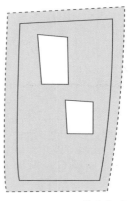

6. Trim away the excess wall fabric leaving a 3/16" seam allowance. Turn the window/wall unit over and trim away the excess window fabric. Stitch the window/wall unit in place.

Secrets to a Great Circle

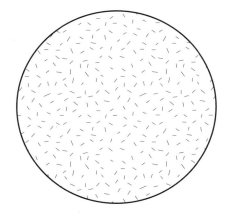

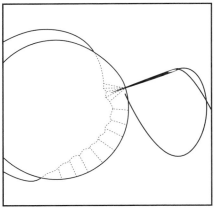

3. Reach in with the tip of your needle and open up the fold. Smooth the curve and stitch.

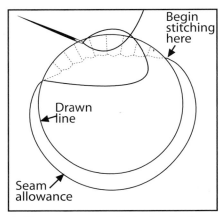

Begin stitching here

Drawn line

Seam allowance

1. Finger press all circles before you pin them in place. Begin sewing. Take it one stitch at a time.

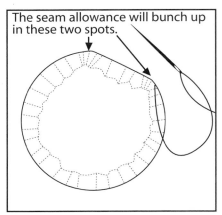

The seam allowance will bunch up in these two spots.

4. The last 1/4"-3/8" of the circle will want to turn under all at once. When you turn it under this part of the circle will flatten out.

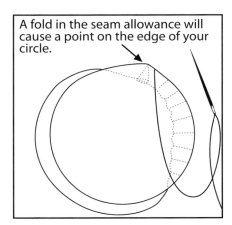

A fold in the seam allowance will cause a point on the edge of your circle.

2. As you turn under a curve the seam allowance can fold over itself and cause a point in the outer edge.

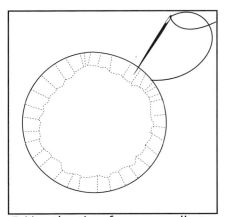

5. Use the tip of your needle to smooth out the bunched seam allowance and to pull the flattened part of the circle into a more round shape.

Setting together All Around the Neighborhood

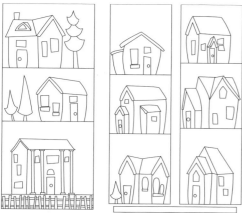

1. Press and then trim the blocks to size. Sew the house blocks together into three vertical rows.

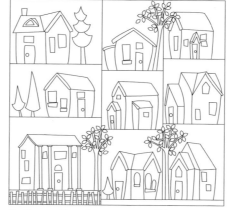

3. Sew the last row of houses to the quilt center. Applique Tree #3 in place.

2. Sew the two rows of houses on the right together. Applique Trees #1 and #2 in place. Open any seam at the base of a tree so that you can hide the bottom of the tree trunk. Sew the seam back together after the tree trunk is appliqued. Attach the grass strip to the bottom of Blocks #9 and #10.

4. Attach the inner borders.
Press and trim the Outer Borders and the Border Corner Blocks. Sew these border units to the quilt as shown.

The Patterns

All Around the Neighborhood
Block #1

15" wide x 11" tall, finished size
Cut your background 17" x 13".

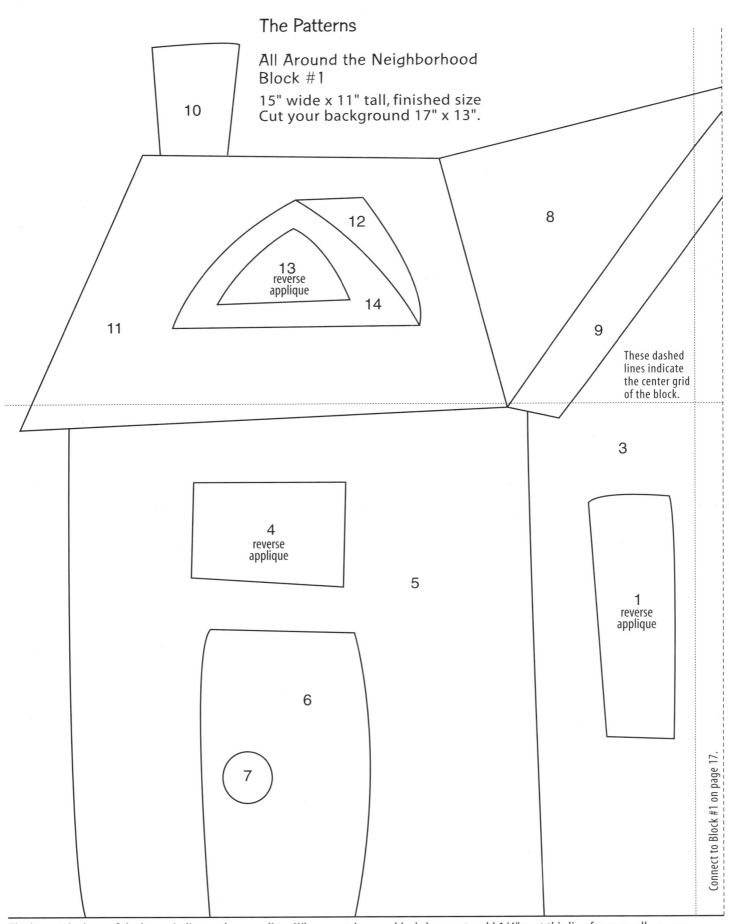

These dashed lines indicate the center grid of the block.

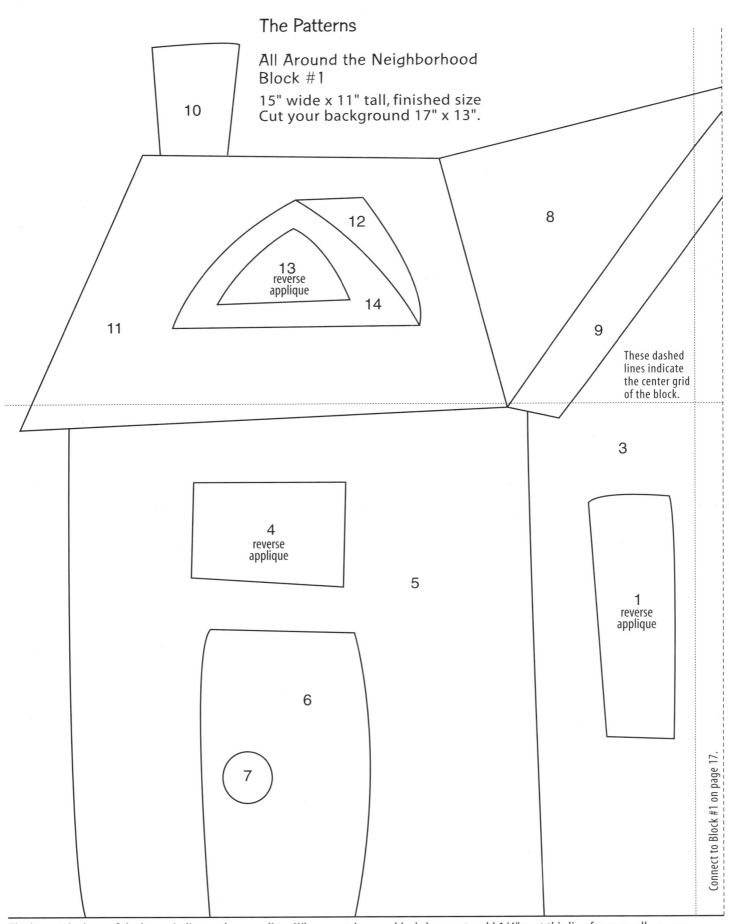10

Connect to Block #1 on page 17.

The line at the base of the house indicates the seam line. When you trim your block, be sure to add 1/4" past this line for seam allowance.

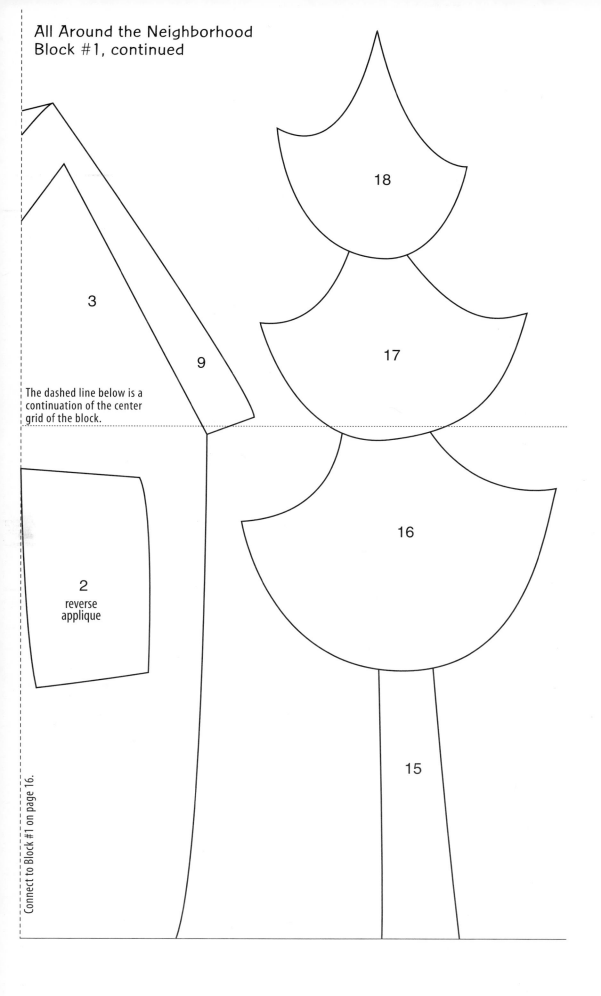

3

9

The dashed line below is a
continuation of the center
grid of the block.

18

17

16

15

2
reverse
applique

Connect to Block #1 on page 16.

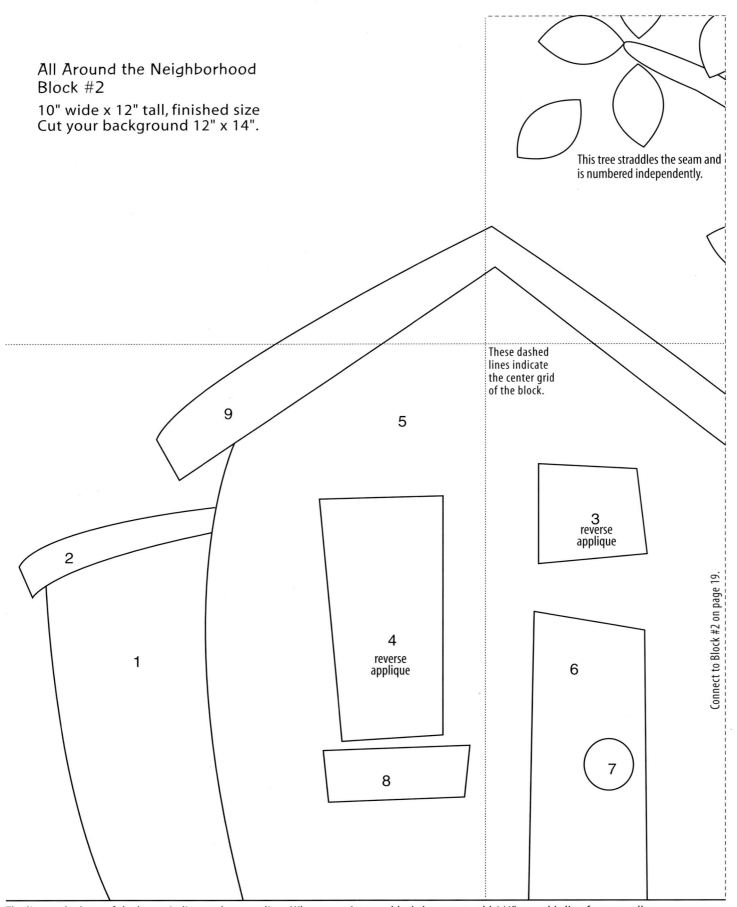

All Around the Neighborhood
Block #2

10" wide x 12" tall, finished size
Cut your background 12" x 14".

This tree straddles the seam and is numbered independently.

These dashed lines indicate the center grid of the block.

9

5

2

3
reverse
applique

1

4
reverse
applique

6

8

7

Connect to Block #2 on page 19.

The line at the base of the house indicates the seam line. When you trim your block, be sure to add 1/4" past this line for seam allowance.

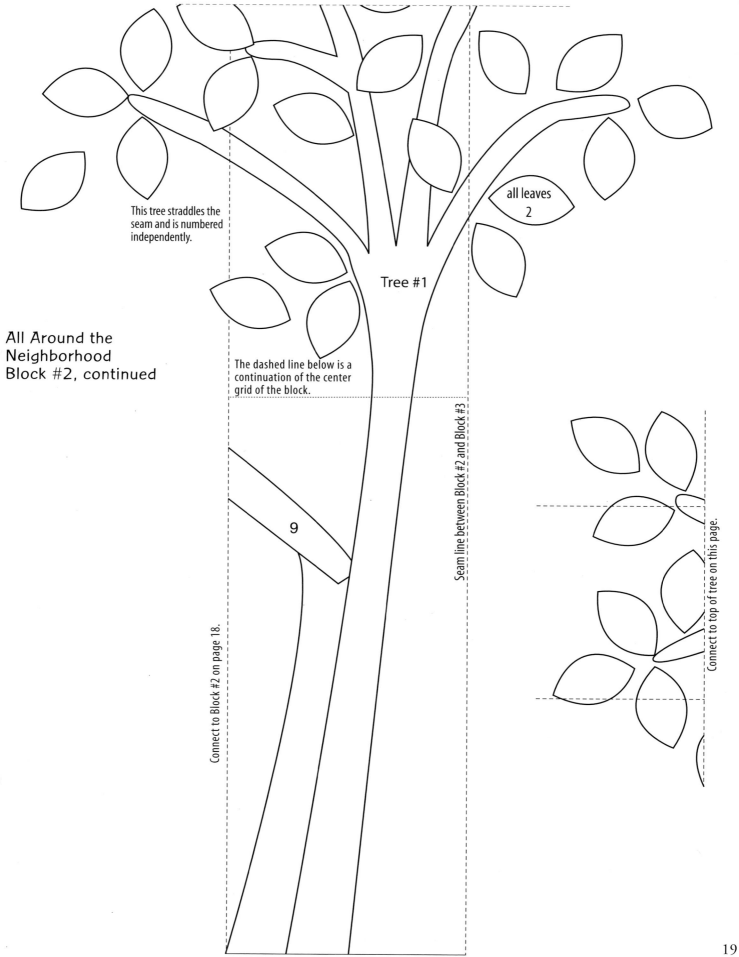

This tree straddles the seam and is numbered independently.

all leaves 2

Tree #1

All Around the Neighborhood Block #2, continued

The dashed line below is a continuation of the center grid of the block.

9

Connect to Block #2 on page 18.

Seam line between Block #2 and Block #3

Connect to top of tree on this page.

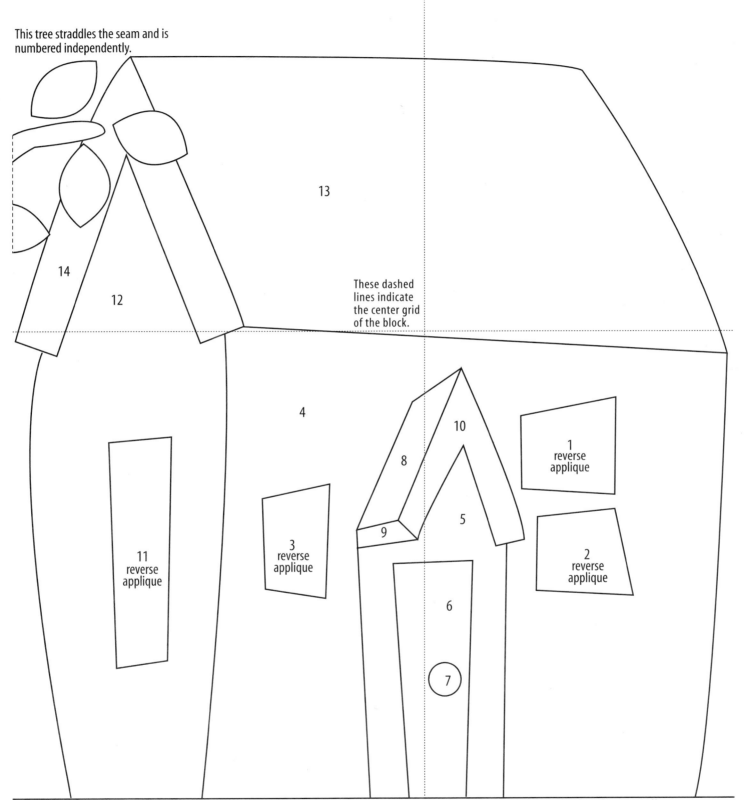

All Around the Neighborhood
Block #3

10" wide x 10" tall, finished size
Cut your background 12" square.

This tree straddles the seam and is numbered independently.

These dashed lines indicate the center grid of the block.

13

14

12

4

10

8

9

5

6

7

1
reverse
applique

2
reverse
applique

3
reverse
applique

11
reverse
applique

The line at the base of the house indicates the seam line. When you trim your block, be sure to add 1/4" past this line for seam allowance.

All Around the Neighborhood
Block #4

15" wide x 9" tall, finished size
Cut your background 17" x 11".

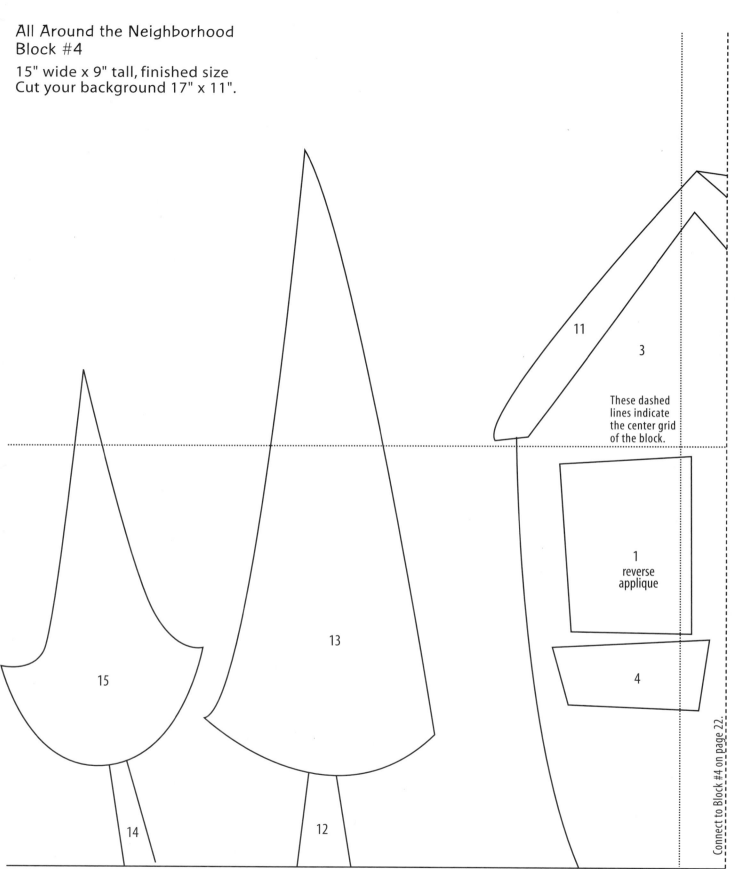

11

3

These dashed
lines indicate
the center grid
of the block.

1
reverse
applique

4

13

15

14

12

Connect to Block #4 on page 22.

The line at the base of the house indicates the seam line. When you trim your block, be sure to add 1/4" past this line for seam allowance.

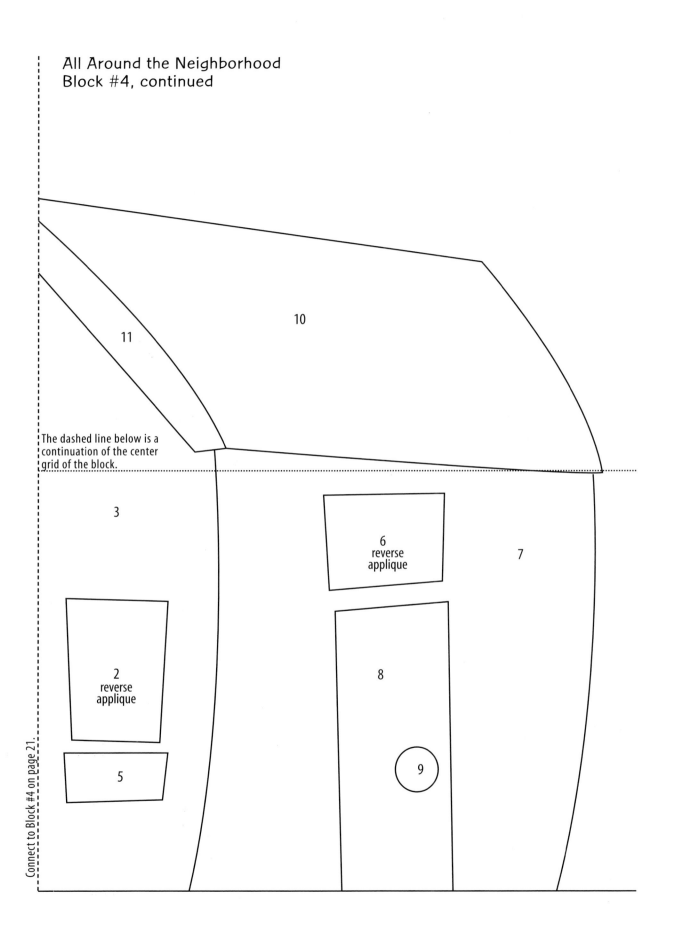

All Around the Neighborhood
Block #4, continued

11

10

The dashed line below is a
continuation of the center
grid of the block.

3

6
reverse
applique

7

2
reverse
applique

8

5

9

Connect to Block #4 on page 21.

All Around the Neighborhood
Block #5

10" wide x 10" tall, finished size
Cut your background 12" square.

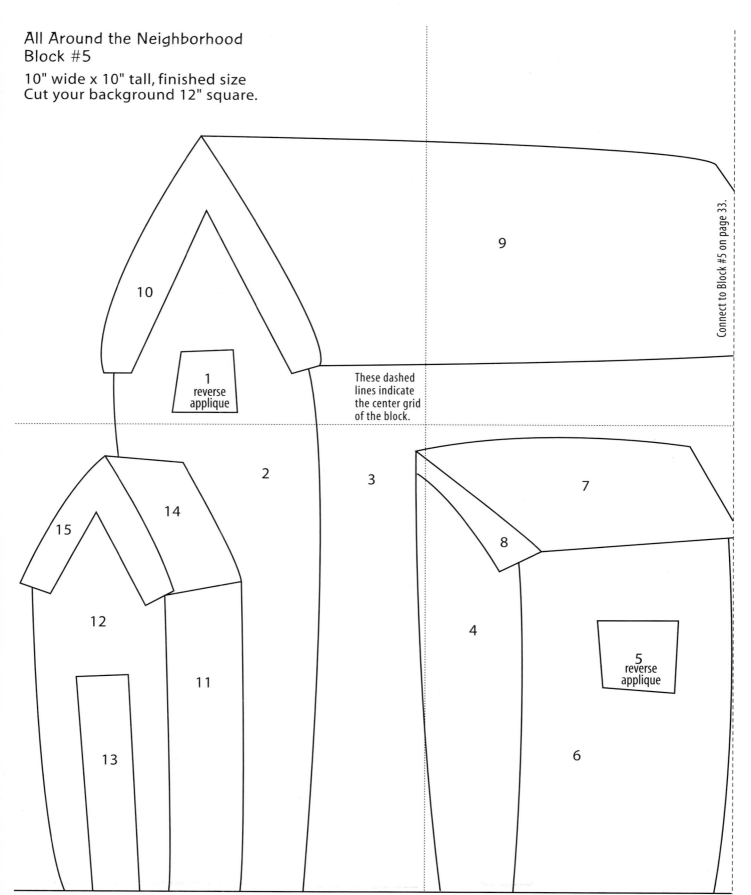

Connect to Block #5 on page 33.

These dashed lines indicate the center grid of the block.

The line at the base of the house indicates the seam line. When you trim your block, be sure to add 1/4" past this line for seam allowance.

All Around the Neighborhood
Block #6

10" wide x 11" tall, finished size
Cut your background 12" x 13".

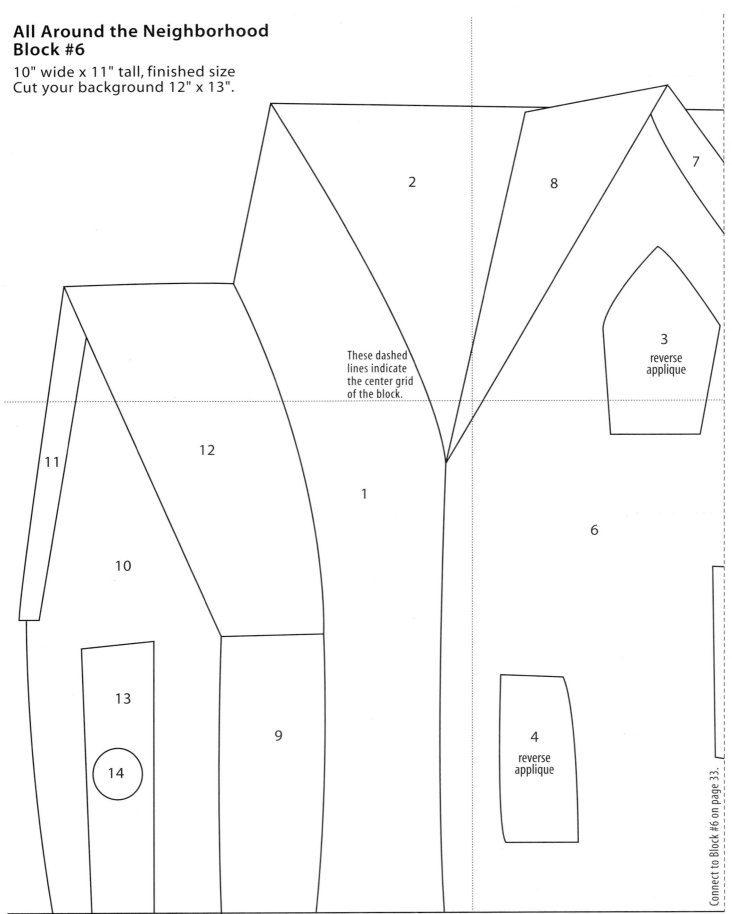

These dashed lines indicate the center grid of the block.

2

8

7

3
reverse applique

11

12

1

10

6

13

14

9

4
reverse applique

Connect to Block #6 on page 33.

The line at the base of the house indicates the seam line. When you trim your block, be sure to add 1/4" past this line for seam allowance.

All Around the Neighborhood hangs above this wonderful iron day bed while
Windows in the Cabin is handy to snuggle up with for a restful nap with your teddy bears!
See instructions beginning on page 10 and on page 64.

Windows in the Cabin keeps Linda warm on her deck where she can stitch with the mountains in sight.
The Little Log Bungalows table runner brings a dash of color to the white wicker table.
See instructions beginning on page 64 and on page 63.

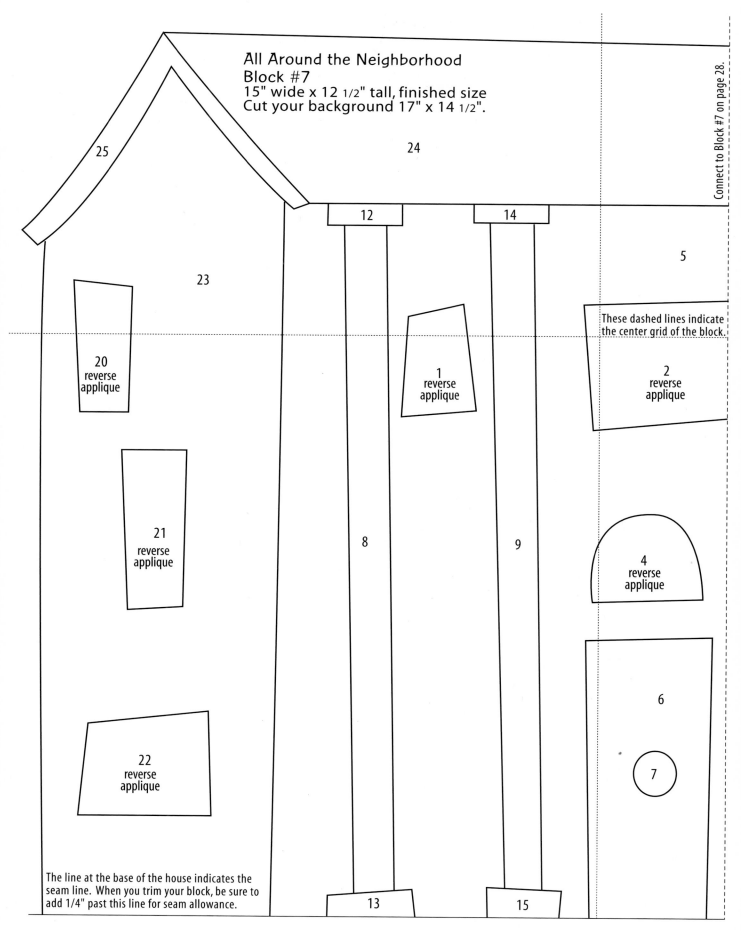

All Around the Neighborhood
Block #7
15" wide x 12 1/2" tall, finished size
Cut your background 17" x 14 1/2".

25

24

Connect to Block #7 on page 28.

12

14

5

23

These dashed lines indicate
the center grid of the block.

20
reverse
applique

1
reverse
applique

2
reverse
applique

21
reverse
applique

8

9

4
reverse
applique

6

22
reverse
applique

7

13

15

The line at the base of the house indicates the
seam line. When you trim your block, be sure to
add 1/4" past this line for seam allowance.

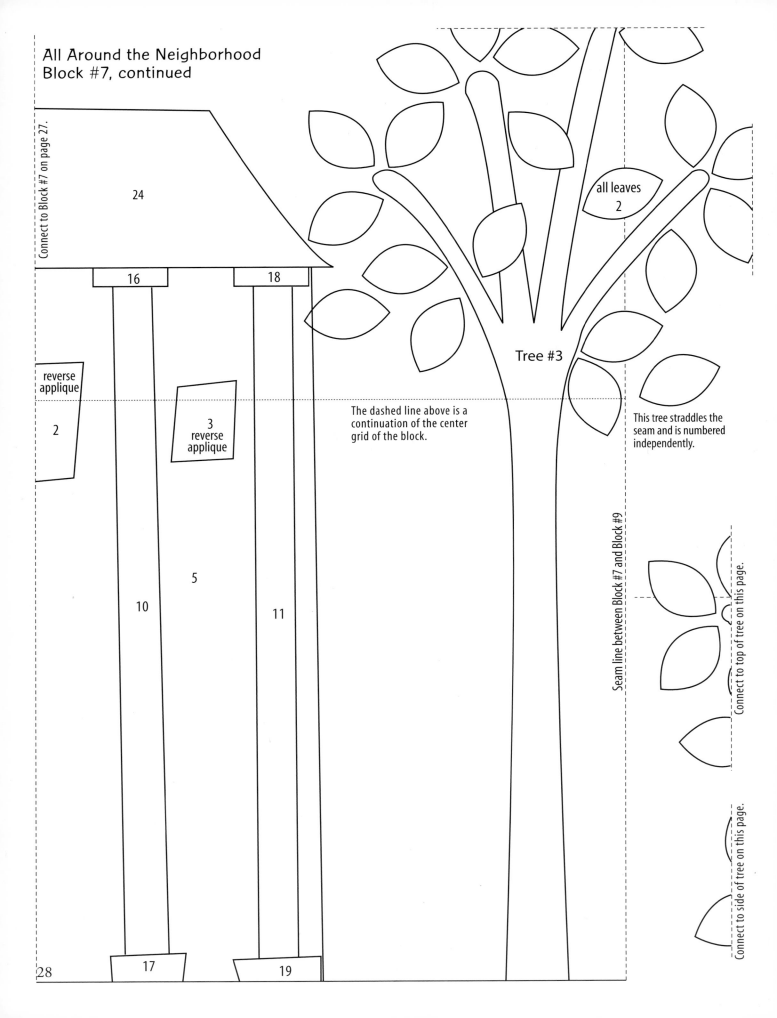

Connect to Block #7 on page 27.

24

16

18

reverse
applique

2

3
reverse
applique

5

10

11

17

19

all leaves
2

Tree #3

The dashed line above is a
continuation of the center
grid of the block.

This tree straddles the
seam and is numbered
independently.

Seam line between Block #7 and Block #9

Connect to top of tree on this page.

Connect to side of tree on this page.

All Around the Neighborhood
Block #8

15" wide x 2 1/2" tall, finished size
Cut your background 17" x 4 1/2".
Block #8 is in two parts on this page.

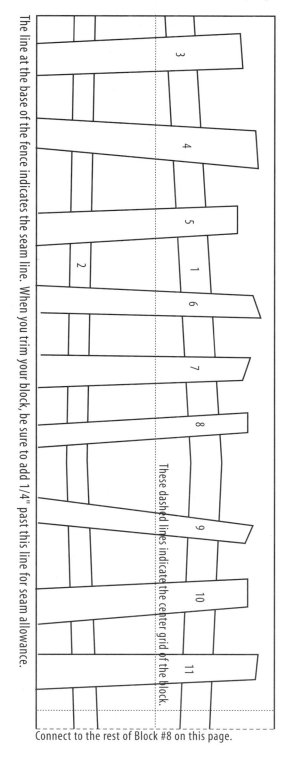

The line at the base of the fence indicates the seam line. When you trim your block, be sure to add 1/4" past this line for seam allowance.

These dashed lines indicate the center grid of the block.

Connect to the rest of Block #8 on this page.

Connect to the other side of Block #8 on this page.

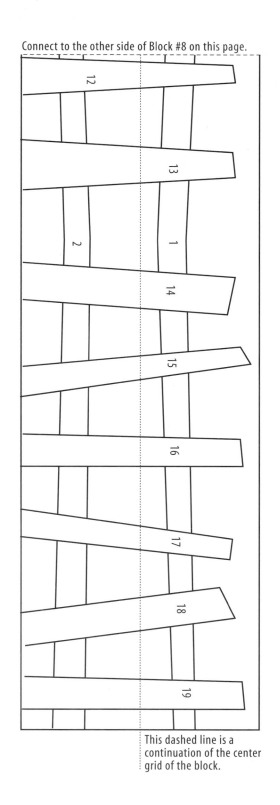

This dashed line is a continuation of the center grid of the block.

All Around the Neighborhood
Block #9

10" wide x 12" tall, finished size
Cut your background 12" x 14".

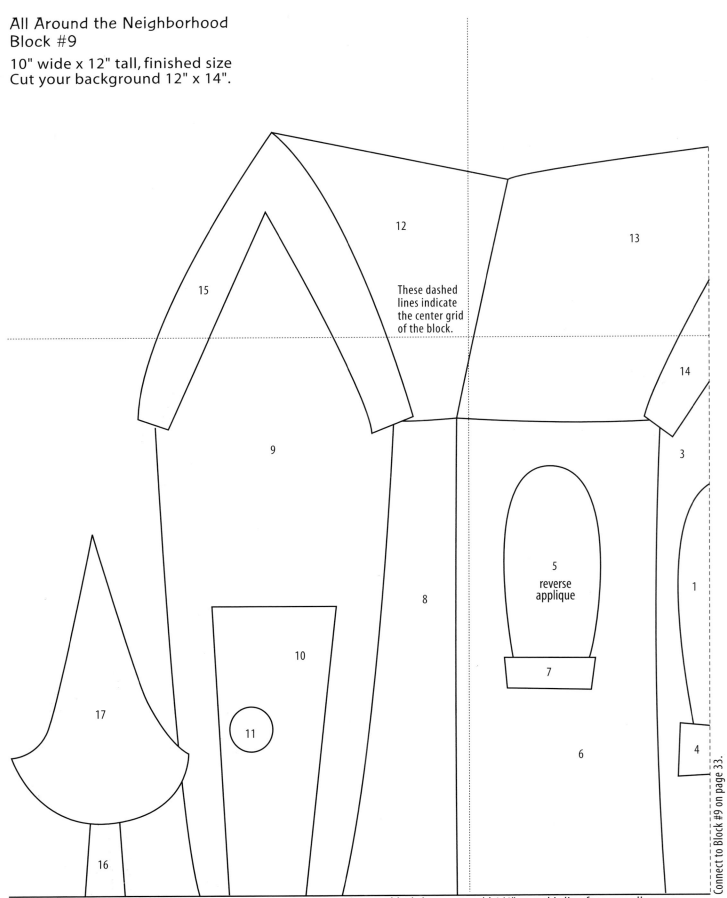

12

13

These dashed
lines indicate
the center grid
of the block.

15

14

9

3

5

reverse
applique

8

1

10

7

17

11

6

4

16

The line at the base of the house indicates the seam line. When you trim your block, be sure to add 1/4" past this line for seam allowance.

Connect to Block #9 on page 33.

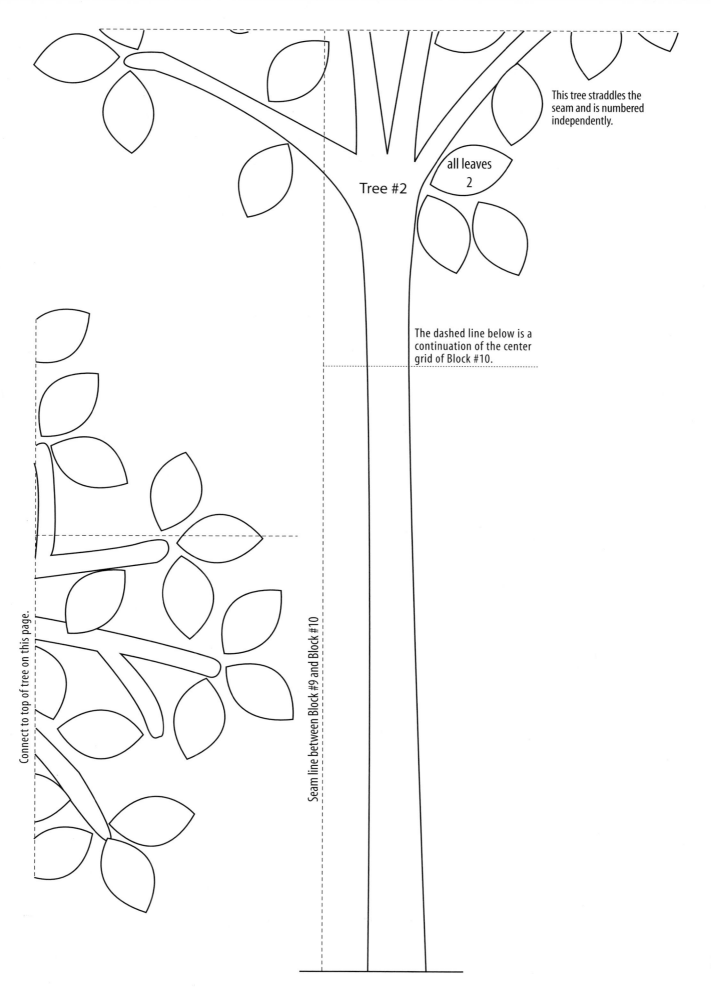

This tree straddles the seam and is numbered independently.

Tree #2

all leaves
2

The dashed line below is a continuation of the center grid of Block #10.

Connect to top of tree on this page.

Seam line between Block #9 and Block #10

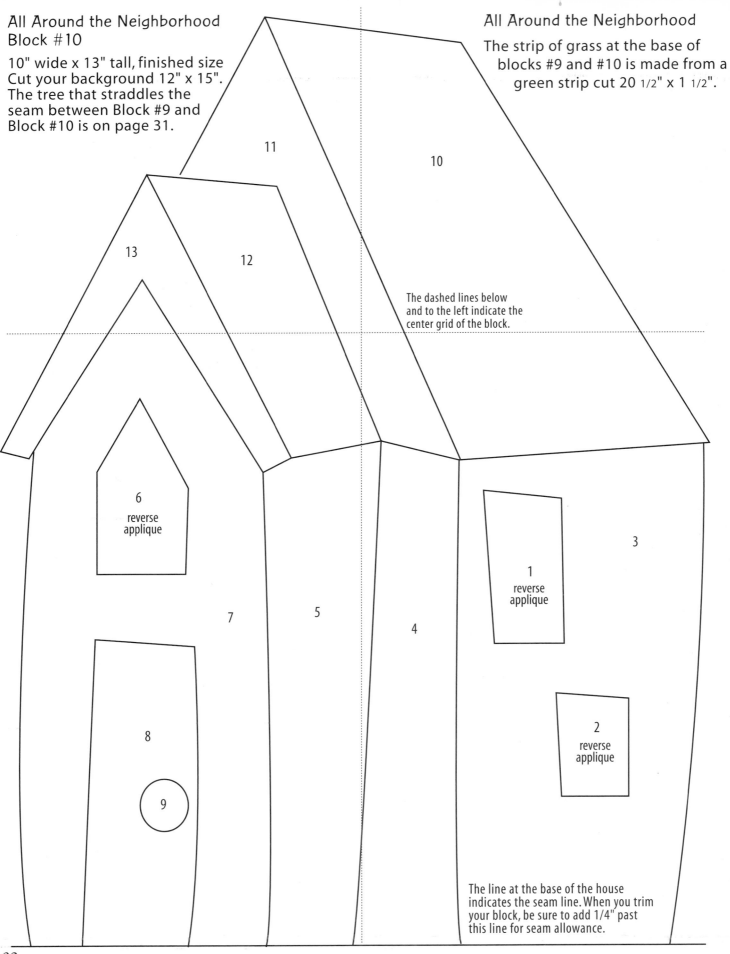

All Around the Neighborhood
Block #10

10" wide x 13" tall, finished size
Cut your background 12" x 15".
The tree that straddles the
seam between Block #9 and
Block #10 is on page 31.

All Around the Neighborhood

The strip of grass at the base of
blocks #9 and #10 is made from a
green strip cut 20 1/2" x 1 1/2".

11

10

13

12

The dashed lines below
and to the left indicate the
center grid of the block.

6
reverse
applique

3

1
reverse
applique

7

5

4

2
reverse
applique

8

9

The line at the base of the house
indicates the seam line. When you trim
your block, be sure to add 1/4" past
this line for seam allowance.

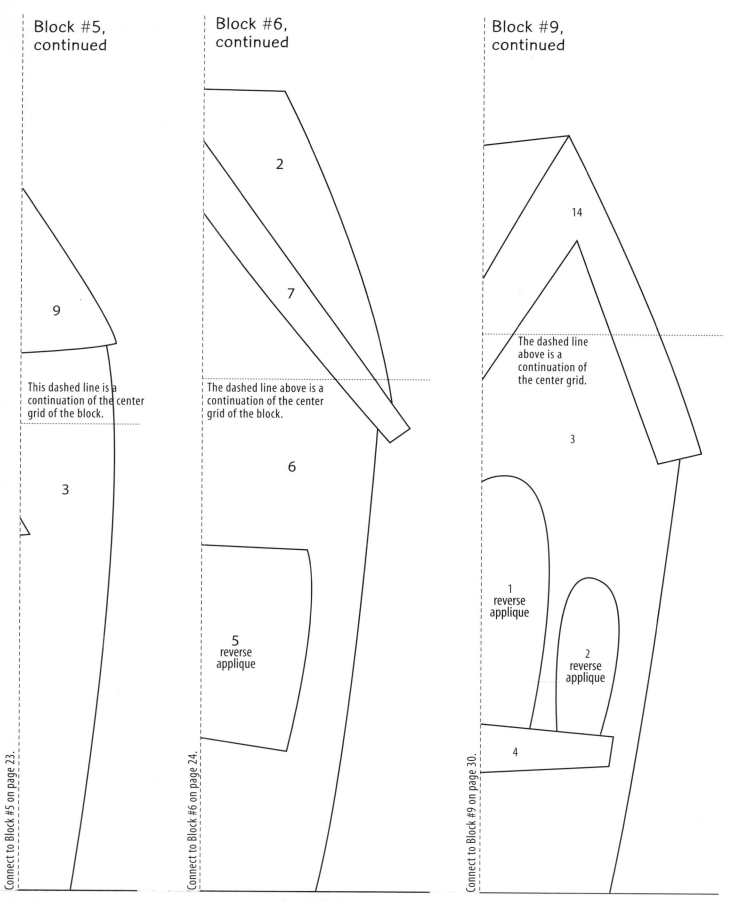

Block #5, continued

Block #6, continued

Block #9, continued

9

This dashed line is a continuation of the center grid of the block.

3

2

7

The dashed line above is a continuation of the center grid of the block.

6

5
reverse applique

14

The dashed line above is a continuation of the center grid.

3

1
reverse applique

2
reverse applique

4

Connect to Block #5 on page 23.

Connect to Block #6 on page 24.

Connect to Block #9 on page 30.

All Around the Neighborhood Outer Border

Make four appliqued border strips,
36" wide x 7 1/2" tall, finished size.
Cut your background 38" x 9 1/2".

Each child is numbered individually.
Draw the faces with a permanent marker.

This dashed line is
a continuation of
the center grid of
the block.

Connect to Border segment on page 35.
Match the letters in the corner.
AA

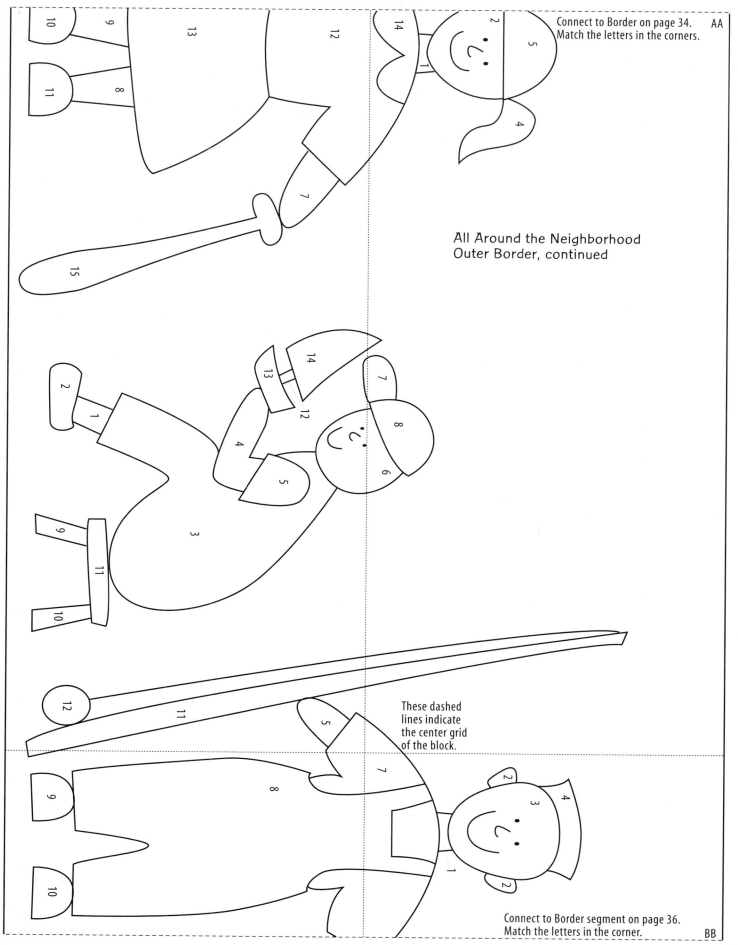

Connect to Border on page 34.
Match the letters in the corners. AA

All Around the Neighborhood
Outer Border, continued

These dashed
lines indicate
the center grid
of the block.

Connect to Border segment on page 36.
Match the letters in the corner. BB

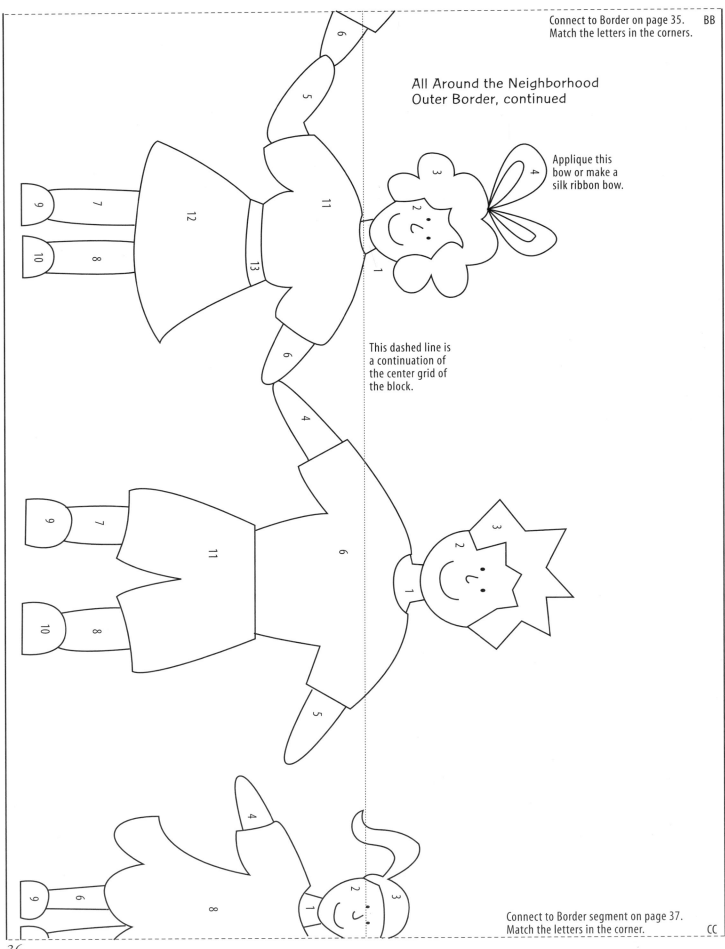

Connect to Border on page 35.
Match the letters in the corners. BB

All Around the Neighborhood
Outer Border, continued

Applique this bow or make a silk ribbon bow.

This dashed line is a continuation of the center grid of the block.

Connect to Border segment on page 37.
Match the letters in the corner. CC

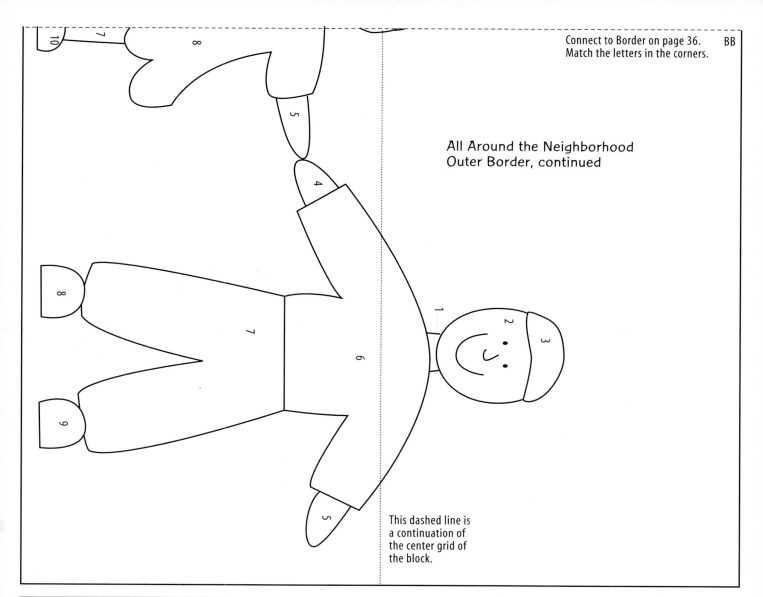

**All Around the Neighborhood
Outer Border, continued**

This dashed line is
a continuation of
the center grid of
the block.

Dress up your bed the easy way!

Buy plain pillow shams in colors
that match your bed quilt. Applique
a design on them. We think that
some of the kids from the border of
All Around the Neighborhood work
great here.

Border Corner Block

7 1/2" square, finished size
Cut your background 9 1/2" square.
Make four of these blocks.

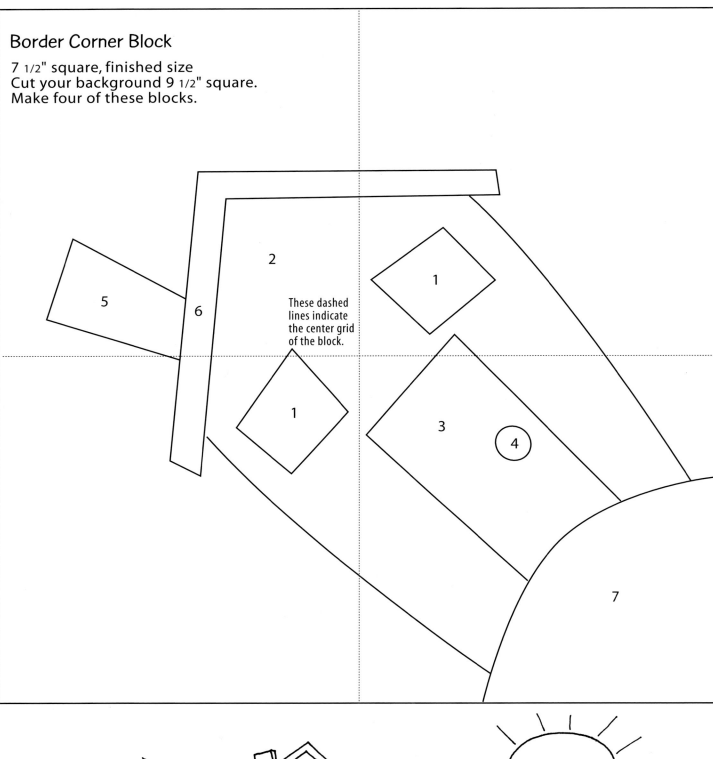

These dashed lines indicate the center grid of the block.

The Blessing Sampler greets visitors in the entry area of Linda's house in the mountains.
See instructions beginning on page 41.

Don't forget to decorate the bathroom with quilts!
The well-loved blessing on The Blessing Sampler reminds those who read it of God's place in our hearts.
See instructions beginning on page 41.

The Blessing Sampler

Yardage for this 26" x 31" wallhanging

Yellow Background: 2/3 yard
Deep Red Letters: 1/4 yard
Vine: 1/2 yard
Periwinkle Inner Border: 1/4 yard
Outer Border: 5/8 yard
Binding: one 18" square to make a continuous bias strip 2" wide
Cording: one 16" square to make a continuous bias strip 1 1/2" wide
Piping Cord: 3 1/4 yards
Backing and Sleeve: 3/4 yard
You will need a variety of small pieces of fabric for your applique.

Cut your fabric as follows:
Background .... 20" x 25"
Letter Fabric .... 8" x 20"
Inner Border, cut one each top & bottom .... 1 1/2" x 28 1/2"
Inner Border, cut two sides .... 1 1/2" x 33 1/2"
Outer Border, cut one each top & bottom .... 4 1/2" x 28 1/2"
Outer Border, cut two sides.. 4 1/2" x 33 1/2"
Vine, cut eight strips on the true bias .... 1 1/2" x 18"

Reverse applique the letters

The letters are stitched first. Prepare your overlay. Press the center grid into
your background fabric. Place your background fabric over the blessing on
the pattern in the proper location. You will need to trace or copy the pattern
as it will be hard to use while bound in the book. If your background fabric is
dark, you will need a light box. Trace the outline of the letters onto your
background. Refer to the "Reverse Appliqued Letters and Numbers" instructions on page 42.

Assemble the wallhanging

Complete the applique in the center block. Press it and trim it to size. Sew an
inner border strip to an outer border strip, matching the lengths. Repeat for
all sides. Sew the borders to the center block, mitering the corners. The outer
border is 1" wider at this point than it will be when the wallhanging is
finished.

Applique the vine, using the seam line between the inner and outer border as
a placement guide on your overlay. Press the wallhanging. Trim the outer
border to 3 1/4" wide. Finish the wallhanging as described in the general
instructions.

Reverse Applique Letters & Numbers

The Blessing Sampler

Trace the letters and date onto your background. If your fabric is too dark to see the pattern through, use a light box. An alphabet in all capital letters and numbers 0-9 can be found on page 52 so that you can put your own initials and date on your quilt. To stitch, follow directions 2-5 at right.

These smaller letters and numbers require a little more patience. Here are some tips:

Be sure to choose a tightly woven fabric for your background.

Take smaller stitches.

Don't overwork your turned-under seam allowance as this will cause fraying.

Use sharp embroidery scissors — dull or too large scissors will chew up your fabric.

This is your quilt — you can embroider the letters and numbers if you want to!

There Goes the Neighborhood

1. Make templates for the letters and numbers. Use the overlay to position the letter templates over the primary border background fabric. Trace around the templates. Both fabrics are right side up.

2. Lay the primary border fabric over a piece of letter fabric that is large enough to accommodate the entire word.

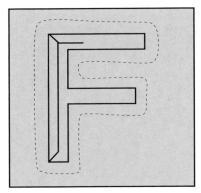

3. Baste around the letters. Keep your basting about 3/8" away from the drawn edges of the letters.

4. Cut (through the primary border fabric only) down the center of the long axis of the "F". Clip the corners as shown. Do not cut the whole letter. Begin sewing.

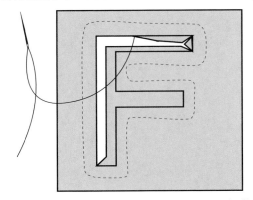

5. Continue clipping and sewing until all of the letters and numbers are complete.

42

Reverse Appliqued Window with a Sash

1. Place the window sash template on top of the window sash fabric, both right sides up. Be sure to lay the template on the fabric so that most of the edges will be on the diagonal grain of the fabric. Trace the stem.

2. Cut the stem out of the bigger piece of stem fabric. Leave 1" or more of excess fabric around the traced stem. Finger press the drawn line under.

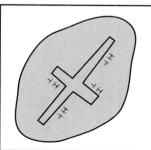

3. Finger press the window sash. Pin it to a piece of fabric that will be the inside of the window.

4. Trim away the excess fabric leaving an 1/8" seam allowance and sew 1/4 of the window sash down at a time. Clip the inner point.

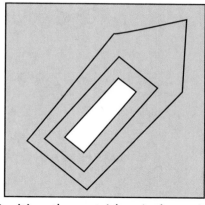

5. Position the outside window trim template on its fabric. Trace around it. Finger press the inside of the window on the drawn lines. Cut a rectangle out of the center, leaving a scant 3/16" seam allowance.

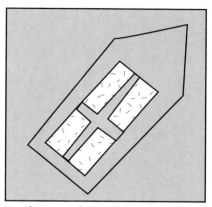

6. Use the overlay to position the window trim over the window sash unit. Reverse applique the inside of the window, revealing the window sash unit.

7. Turn the unit over and cut away all excess fabric from the window sash. Be sure to leave a 3/16" seam allowance to the outside of the window. Sew it in place as a unit.

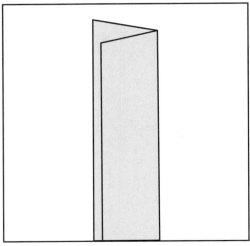

1. Cut eight strips on the bias grain of the fabric 1 1/2" x 18". Press them in half, right sides out.

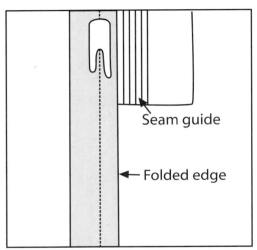

Seam guide

← Folded edge

2. Place the folded edge of each of the bias strips against the seam 1/4" seam guide of your sewing machine and sew.

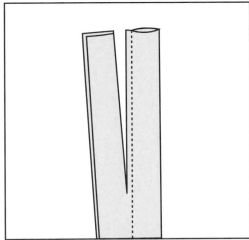

3. Trim away excess fabric, leaving a very scant seam allowance.

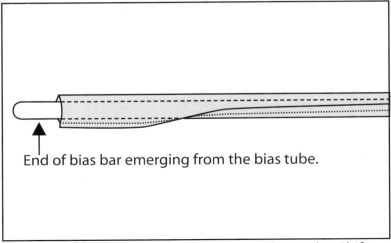

End of bias bar emerging from the bias tube.

4. Insert the 1/4" bias bar into your sewn bias tube. Shift the seam and seam allowance to the back of the bar and press it in place.

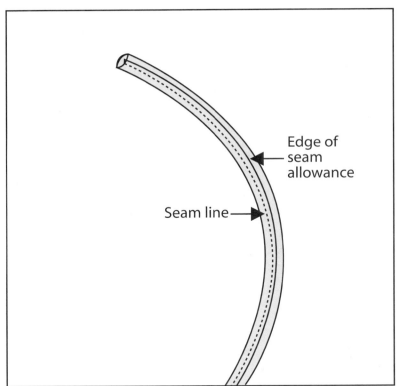

Edge of seam allowance

Seam line →

5. Hold up a finished piece of bias stem. You'll notice that it wants to curve better in one direction than the other. The side closest to the seam line makes the tighter curve. When possible, match this side of the bias stem to the concave side of the stem on your pattern.

The Patterns

The Blessing Sampler
Center block 18" wide x 23" tall, finished size
Cut your background 20" x 25".

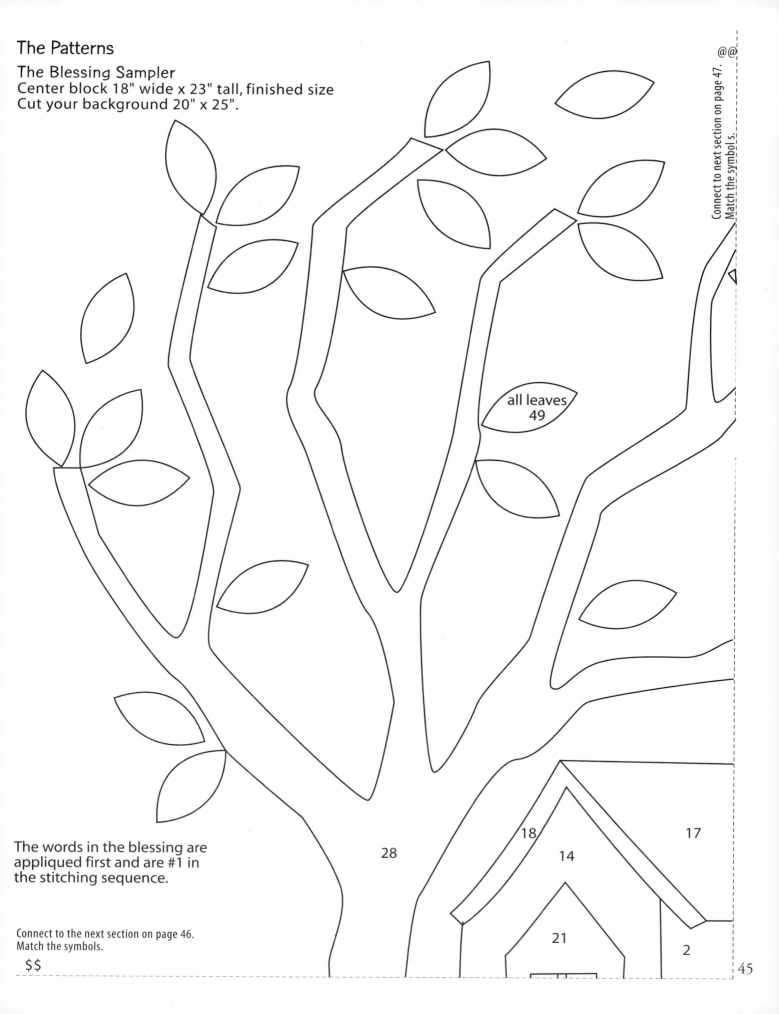

all leaves
49

The words in the blessing are appliqued first and are #1 in the stitching sequence.

28

18

14

17

21

2

Connect to the next section on page 46.
Match the symbols.

$$

Connect to next section on page 47.
Match the symbol s.

@@

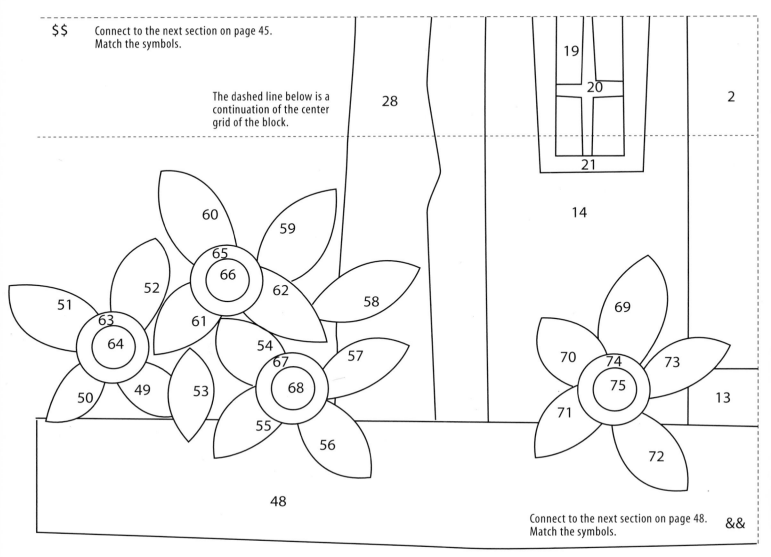

$$ Connect to the next section on page 45.
Match the symbols.

The dashed line below is a
continuation of the center
grid of the block.

19

20

2

28

21

14

60

59

65

66

52

62

58

51

63

64

61

54

57

69

50

49

53

67

68

55

56

70

74

75

73

71

13

48

72

Connect to the next section on page 48.   &&
Match the symbols.

Here's a fast and fun idea:
Frame an applique block for your wall!

We made our blocks to fit ready-made
frames. Cut your backgrounds 4"
wider and taller than the frame's
opening. Applique the design. Press
the block. Stretch the block over a
padded mounting board and secure
the edges to the back of the board.
Put it in the frame, add a cardboard
backing and hanger and it's ready to
hang.

Framed blocks make wonderful gifts!

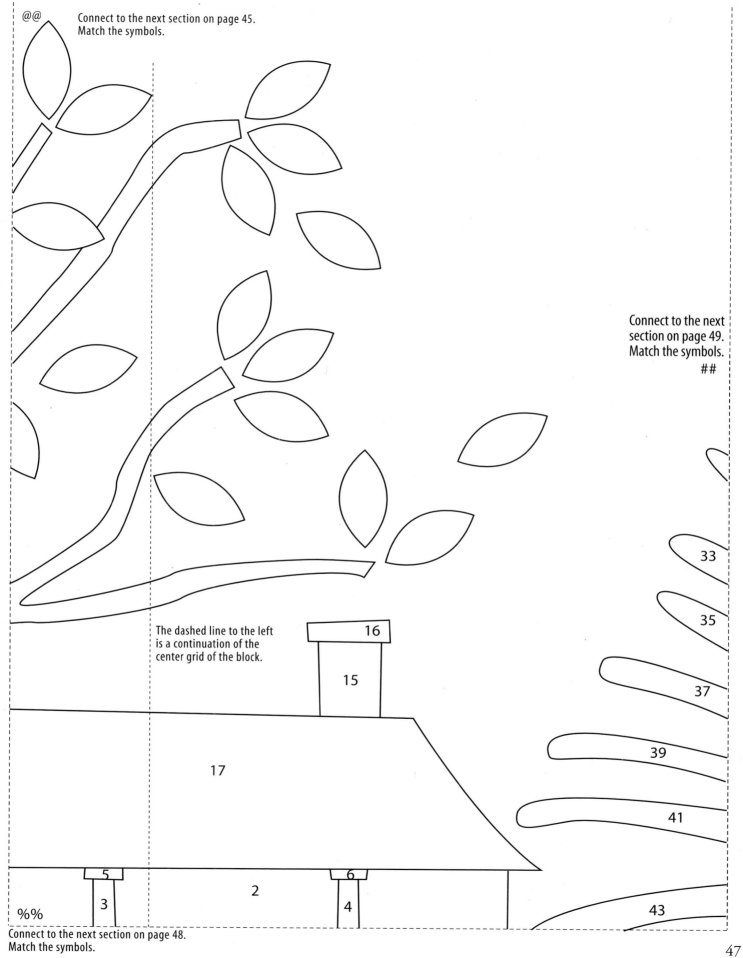

@@

Connect to the next section on page 45.
Match the symbols.

Connect to the next
section on page 49.
Match the symbols.

33

35

37

The dashed line to the left
is a continuation of the
center grid of the block.

16

15

39

17

41

5

6

2

%%

3

4

43

Connect to the next section on page 48.
Match the symbols.

Connect to the next section on page 47.
Match the symbols.

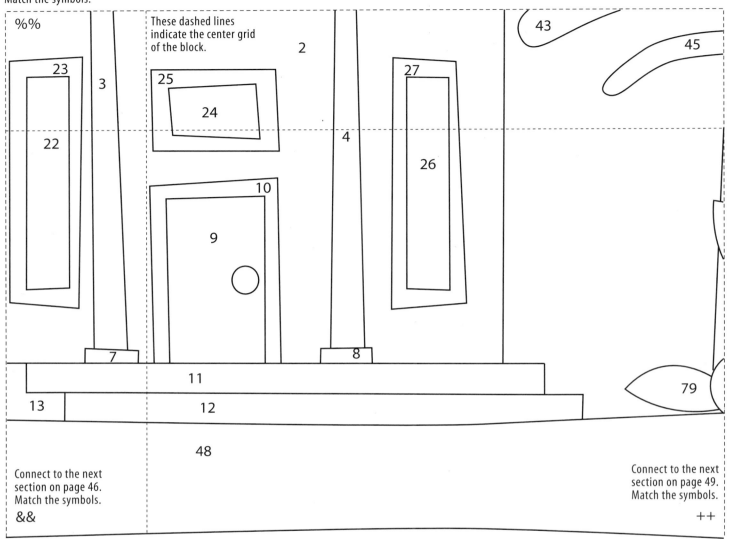

%%

These dashed lines
indicate the center grid
of the block.

2

23

3

25

24

22

4

27

26

10

9

7

8

11

13

12

43

45

79

48

Connect to the next
section on page 46.
Match the symbols.
&&

Connect to the next
section on page 49.
Match the symbols.
++

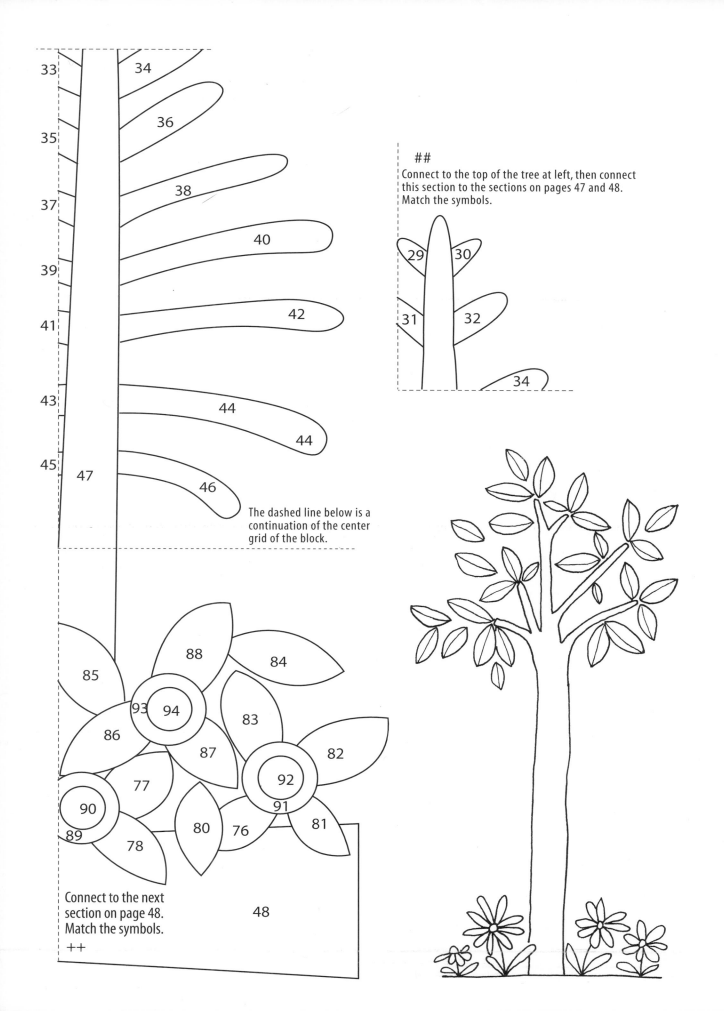

33

34

36

35

38

37

40

39

42

41

43

44

44

45

47

46

The dashed line below is a
continuation of the center
grid of the block.

##
Connect to the top of the tree at left, then connect
this section to the sections on pages 47 and 48.
Match the symbols.

29 30

31 32

34

88

85

84

93 94

83

86

87

82

77

92

90

91

89

80 76

81

78

Connect to the next
section on page 48.
Match the symbols.
++

48

Connect to the next section on page 51.
Match the symbols.

The dashed line above is a continuation of the center grid of the block.

**

This line marks the bottom of piece #48 of *The Blessing Sampler*.

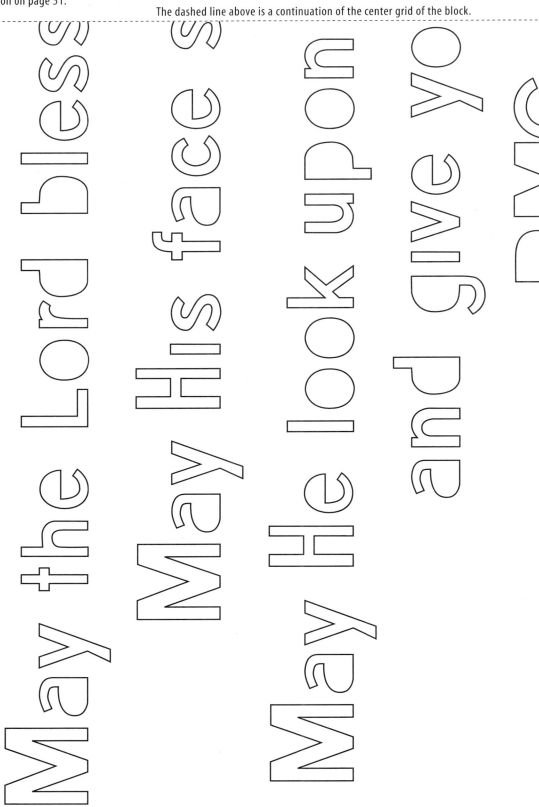

May the Lord bless

May His face s

May He look upon

and give yo

RMG

The words in the blessing are appliqued first and are #1 in the stitching sequence.

This line marks the bottom of piece #48 of The Blessing Sampler.

you and keep you

hine upon you

you with kindness

u His Peace

1999

**

Connect to the next section on page 50.
Match the symbols.

The dashed line above is a continuation of the center grid of the block.

Use the capital letters and numbers below to personalize your own Blessing Sampler.

ABCDEFGHIJ
KLMNOPQR
STUVWXYZ
1234567890

The section of the border (below) from The Blessing Sampler is continued from page 53.

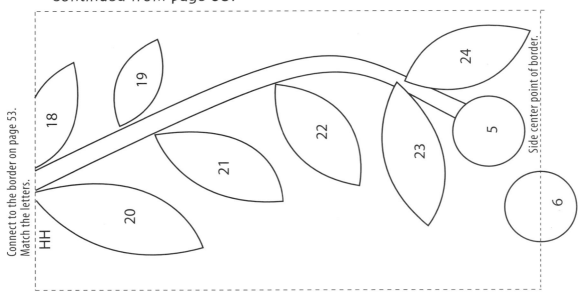

Connect to the border on page 53. Match the letters.

Side center point of border.

HH
18
19
20
21
22
23
24
5
6

This dashed line marks the edge of the quilt.

GG

7

1

26

25

8

9

11

10

2

12

13

14

15

16

17

HH

The outer border is 3" wide, finished, but you will sew 4 1/2" wide border strips to the quilt. After your applique is complete you will trim the border to size. The dashed line on this border pattern is the seam line between the inner and outer border. Use it for proper placement of the outer border applique.

This dashed line marks the seam between the inner and outer border.

Connect to the border above, right.

GG

27

29

28

30

31

32

33

3

4

Top and bottom center point of border.

Connect to the border on page 52.

53

There Goes the Neighborhood

Yardage & Cutting Instructions for the
50" square quilt

Background: Nine 12" squares or
     yardage to total 1 1/8 yards
Sashing: Thirty-six 1 1/2" x 10 1/2" strips or
     yardage to total 5/8 yard
Sashing Corners: Cut thirty-six 1 1/2" squares
Inner Border: 1/4 yard
     Cut four 1 1/2" x 38 1/2" strips
Outer Border: 1 yard
     Cut four strips 8" x 40"
Binding: one 25" square to make a continuous bias
     strip 2 1/2" wide
Cording: one 20" square to make a continuous bias
     strip 1 1/2" wide
Piping Cord (optional): 5 3/4 yards
Backing and Sleeve: 3 1/3 yards
You will need a variety of small pieces of fabric for
your applique.

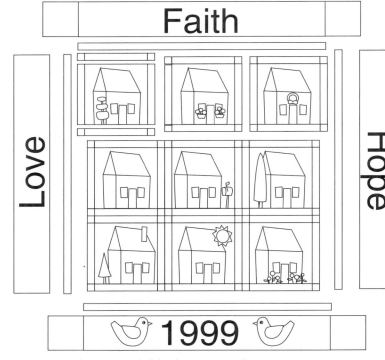

1. Press and trim each block to 10 1/2".
2. Sash each block as shown above.
3. Sew the sashed blocks together into three rows.
4. Sew the rows together.
5. Add the inner border. Miter the corners.
6. Press and trim the outer borders to 6 1/2" x 38 1/2".
Add the outer borders as shown above.

This is the bird pattern for the left side of the
bottom border. Reverse the templates for the
bird on the right side of the border.

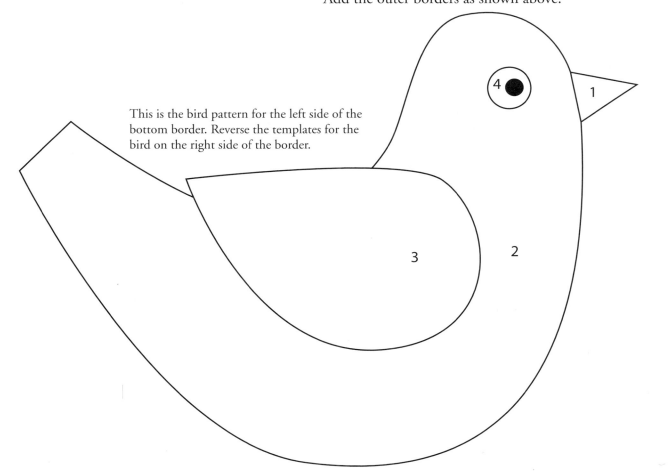

Piece and Applique the Houses

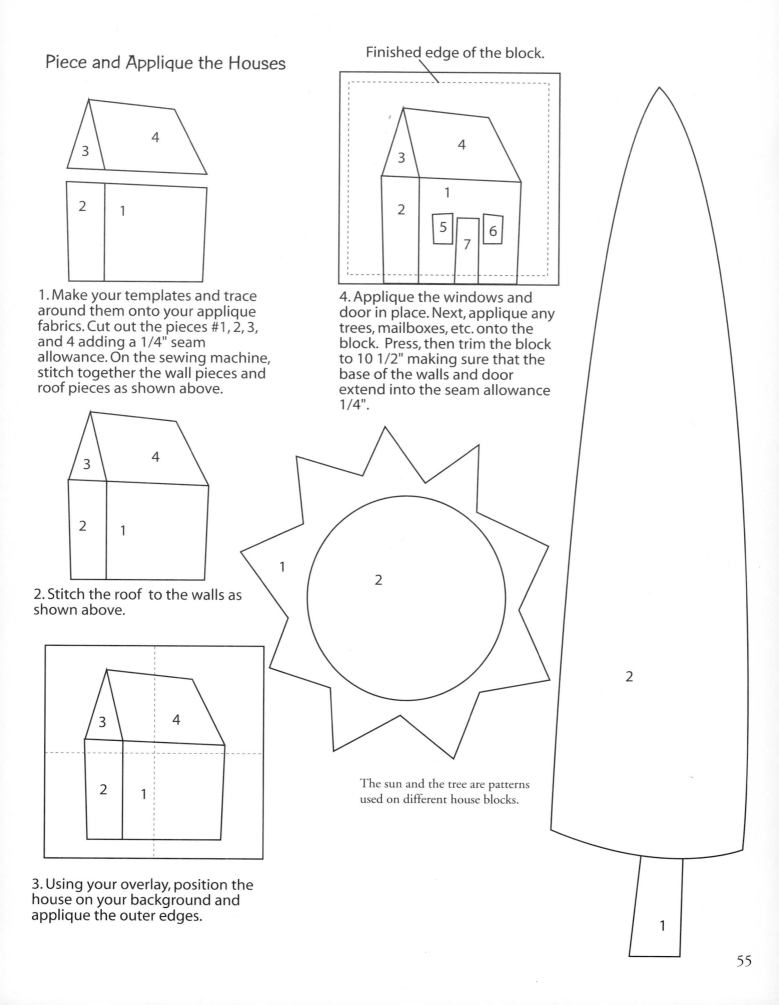

Finished edge of the block.

1. Make your templates and trace around them onto your applique fabrics. Cut out the pieces #1, 2, 3, and 4 adding a 1/4" seam allowance. On the sewing machine, stitch together the wall pieces and roof pieces as shown above.

4. Applique the windows and door in place. Next, applique any trees, mailboxes, etc. onto the block. Press, then trim the block to 10 1/2" making sure that the base of the walls and door extend into the seam allowance 1/4".

2. Stitch the roof to the walls as shown above.

3. Using your overlay, position the house on your background and applique the outer edges.

The sun and the tree are patterns used on different house blocks.

55

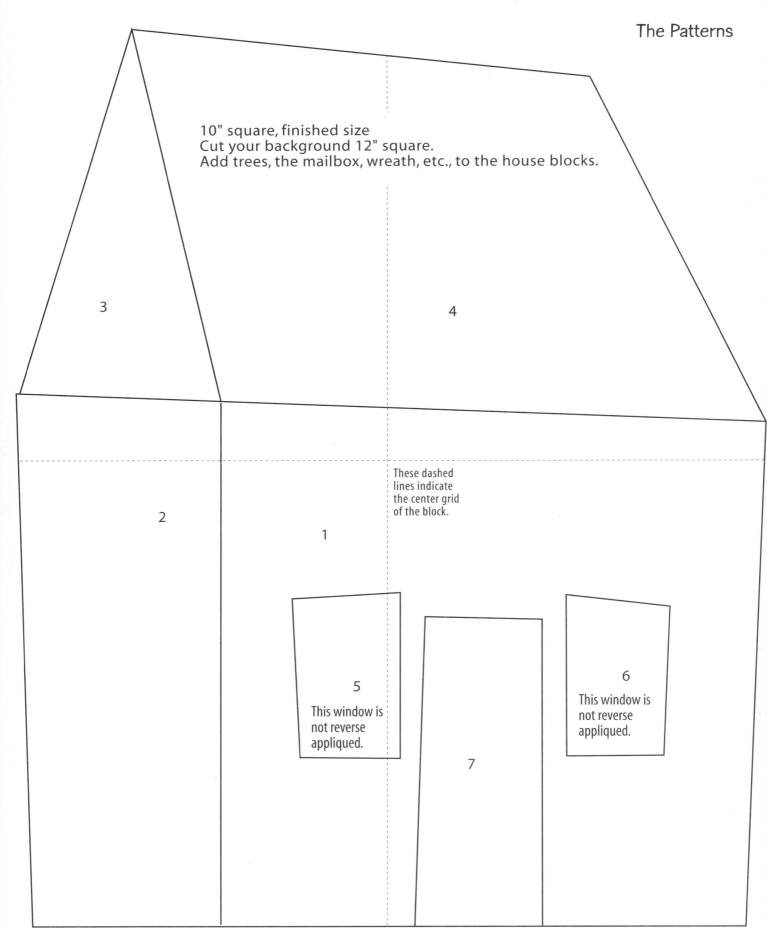

10" square, finished size
Cut your background 12" square.
Add trees, the mailbox, wreath, etc., to the house blocks.

3

4

These dashed
lines indicate
the center grid
of the block.

2

1

5

This window is
not reverse
appliqued.

6

This window is
not reverse
appliqued.

7

The line at the base of the house indicates the seam line. When you trim your block, be sure to add 1/4" past this line for seam allowance.

Little Log Bungalow blocks make a great table runner (shown on Linda's oak buffet) or bed quilt.
Above the buffet two framed blocks from All Around the Neighborhood dress up the wall.
See instructions on page 63 and on page 46.

Windows in the Cabin is up on the design wall in Linda's studio while she works on other projects.
Like many quilters, both Linda and Becky always have something in the works!
See instructions on page 64.

Add trees, the mailbox, wreath, etc., to the house blocks.
Embellish with embroidery, beads, buttons, and more to
make your quilt more interesting!

Applique the window boxes. Our flowers are
glass beads and the leaves are embroidered.

Little Log Bungalows

Yardage

Refer to the color photo on page 57.
Each block finishes 14" wide x 11" tall

Five-block Tablerunner, 14" x 55" finished size
Center Logs: 1/8 yard
Horizontal Logs: a variety of fabrics to total 1/2 yards
Vertical Logs: a variety of fabrics to total 1/2 yards

How about a bed quilt?

This is such a fun block to make that we thought you might be interested in making a bed quilt! Here is the yardage information that you need. There isn't any wiggle room allowed, so you may want a bit more fabric than is called for.

Double-size, 84" x 88"
> Make 48 blocks, 6 blocks wide x 8 tall

Center Logs: 1/4 yard
Horizontal Logs: a variety of fabrics to total 4 1/2 yards
Vertical Logs: a variety of fabrics to total 4 yards

Queen-size, 98" x 88"
> Make 56 blocks, 7 blocks wide x 8 tall

Center Logs: 1/3 yard
Horizontal Logs: a variety of fabrics to total 5 1/4 yards
Vertical Logs: a variety of fabrics to total 4 2/3 yards

King-size, 112" x 88"
> Make 64 blocks, 8 blocks wide x 8 tall

Center Logs: 1/3 yard
Horizontal Logs: a variety of fabrics to total 6 yards
Vertical Logs: a variety of fabrics to total 5 3/8 yards

Cutting Instructions

Center Logs	Cut: Tablerunner	Double	Queen	King
1 1/2" x 4 1/2"	5	48	56	64

Horizontal Logs	Cut: Tablerunner	Double	Queen	King
1 1/2" x 4 1/2"	10	96	112	128
1 1/2" x 6 1/2"	10	96	112	128
1 1/2" x 8 1/2"	10	96	112	128
1 1/2" x 10 1/2"	10	96	112	128
1 1/2" x 12 1/2"	10	96	112	128

Vertical Logs	Cut: Tablerunner	Double	Queen	King
1 1/2" x 3 1/2"	10	96	112	128
1 1/2" x 5 1/2"	10	96	112	128
1 1/2" x 7 1/2"	10	96	112	128
1 1/2" x 9 1/2"	10	96	112	128
1 1/2" x 11 1/2"	10	96	112	128

Assembly Instructions

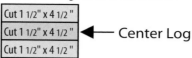

Cut 1 1/2" x 4 1/2"
Cut 1 1/2" x 4 1/2" ← Center Log
Cut 1 1/2" x 4 1/2"

1. Sew the smallest horizontal log to the top and bottom of the center log. Press.

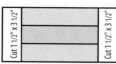

Cut 1 1/2" x 3 1/2"   Cut 1 1/2" x 3 1/2"

2. Sew the smallest vertical log to each side of the center log. Press.

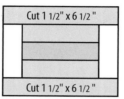

Cut 1 1/2" x 6 1/2"

Cut 1 1/2" x 6 1/2"

3. Sew the next horizontal log to the top and bottom of your growing block. Press.

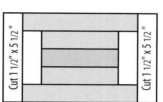

Cut 1 1/2" x 5 1/2"   Cut 1 1/2" x 5 1/2"

4. Continue sewing logs to your block in this manner. Press each pair of logs as you go. The finished size of this block is 14" x 11". Make the number of blocks necessary for your project.

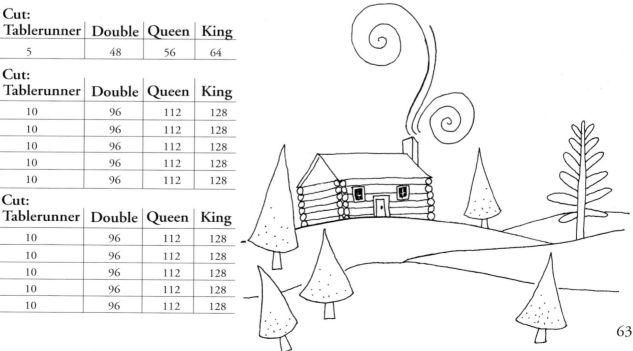

Windows in the Cabin

Yardage & Cutting Instructions

Refer to the color photo on page 58.
Each block finishes 9" square. These blocks are made from a wide varitey of 2" strips that are whacked off at funny angles as you make each block. Yardages are approximate, as some quilters may "whack" more than others. Save the ends of your strips to use in the border.

Throw-size, 57 1/2" square
      Make 36 blocks, 6 blocks wide x 6 tall
Center: a variety of fabrics to total 1/2 yard
Darker Logs: a variety of fabrics to total 2 yards
Brighter Logs: a variety of fabrics to total 2 yards
Inner Border: 1/4 yard cut into eight 3/4" strips
Yellow Window Sash: 1/2 yard cut into 3/4" strips

Double/Queen-size, 93 1/2" square
      Make 100 blocks, 10 blocks wide x 10 tall
Center: a variety of fabrics to total 1 1/4 yards
Darker Logs: a variety of fabrics to total 5 1/2 yards
Brighter Logs: a variety of fabrics to total 5 1/2 yards
Inner Border: 3/8 yard cut into twelve 3/4" strips
Yellow Window Sash: 1 3/8 yards cut into 3/4" strips

King-size, 102 1/2" x 93 1/2"
      Make 110 blocks,11 blocks wide x 10 tall
Center: a variety of fabrics to total 1 1/4 yards
Darker Logs: a variety of fabrics to total 5 3/4 yards
Brighter Logs: a variety of fabrics to total 5 3/4 yards
Inner Border: 3/8 yard cut into twelve 3/4" strips
Yellow Window Sash: 1 1/2 yards cut into 3/4" strips

Assembly Instructions

Cut the center fabric in the appropriate number of 4" squares. "Whack" off the sides at odd angles as shown below. Cut the darker and lighter log fabrics into 2" strips. Work around the center square as shown.

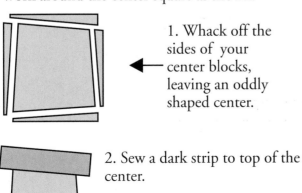

1. Whack off the sides of your center blocks, leaving an oddly shaped center.

2. Sew a dark strip to top of the center.

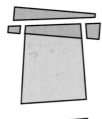

3. Cut off the outer edge of this strip at an angle (any angle!). Cut the ends of the strip even with the sides of the center square.

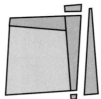

4. Continue adding strips in a clockwise direction around the center square. Trim them all in this manner. Sew two dark strips and then two light strips.

Insert window panes in the blocks at different stages as we did for an interesting look. For example, insert the window pane in four or five of the blocks after you have added one strip to each side of the center square. Insert window panes at later stages, until all or most of the blocks have them.

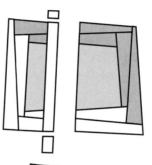

5. When you are ready to insert a window sash, cut the block in half vertically and sew a 3/4" strip of yellow to one side. Trim the ends even with the sides of the block and then sew the two sides of the block together.

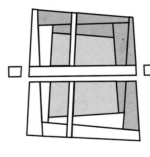

6. Repeat for the horizontal window sash.

7. When all sides are sewn to the block and your window sashes have been inserted, trim your block to 9 1/2" square. Make the appropriate number of blocks for your project.

8. Sew the blocks together to form the center of the quilt. Add the inner border. Sew the leftover ends of the 2" strips together to make four outer border strips. Sew them to the quilt. Finish the quilt as described previously.

studysync®

ASSIGNMENTS   BINDER   LIBRARY

The Power of Communication

Grade 10 Reading & Writing Companion **Unit 1**